Python Programming

&

Data Analysis

-A Beginner's Handbook

V.UMA

ISBN: 9781699799321

DEDICATION

This book is dedicated to my husband, Baskar, and to my children, Hamsika and Nandita.

Contents

Preface

Thank you for purchasing this book. This handbook will help you explore, harness, and gain appreciation of the competencies and features of Python. This book contains several examples that would enable you to learn Python Programming swiftly and commendably.

Python is a high-level, interpreted and general-purpose dynamic programming language. It uses concise and easy-to-learn syntax which enables programmers to develop more complex programs in a much shorter time. This book provides all essential programming concepts and information you need to start developing your own Python program. The book provides a comprehensive walk-through of Python programming in a clear, straightforward manner. Important concepts are introduced with relevant examples, explanations and comments.

This book also provides a gentle introduction to the Pyplot, Numpy and Pandas modules. This will help you start your Data Analyst career.

All the examples provided in this book have been executed successfully on ipython (Jupyter) notebook with Python3. You are hereby instructed to implement the code in the same platform for successful execution and better understanding.

1.Introduction

- Python is a general-purpose, high level, object oriented programming language. It is an easy to learn, free and open source programming language.
- It was created by Guido van Rossum, and released in 1991.
- It works on different platforms (Windows, Mac, Linux, Raspberry Pi, etc).
- Python is used in web development, machine learning, data analysis, scripting, game development etc.
- It has best packages for Artificial Intelligence (AI) viz. matplotlib (plotting library) , numpy, scipy (libraries for performing scientific calculations), scikit-learn (machine learning, data science library) and tensorflow (deep learning library). It is very easy to implement AI algorithms using Python.
- ipython notebook also known as Jupyter notebook is an interactive(code with content) computational environment in which data analysis, modelling and sharing of documents can be performed.
- Python and R are both open-source programming languages with a large community. R is mainly used for statistical analysis while Python provides a more general approach to data science.
- There are two major Python versions- **Python 2 and Python 3**.

- Python can be obtained from the Python Software Foundation website at python.org. Typically, that involves downloading the appropriate installer for your operating system and running it on your machine.

- The open-source Anaconda Distribution is the easiest way to perform Python/R data science and machine learning on Linux, Windows, and Mac OS X.

This book first introduces the basic concepts in Python. In the later chapters, Pyplot, Numpy and Pandas modules are discussed. These chapters would enable the reader to understand the libraries that are widely used in data analysis. The programs given in this book have been implemented and tested on ipython notebook with Python3.

2. Keywords, Identifiers and Variables

2.1 KEYWORDS

- ➢ Refers to reserved words which have special meaning.
- ➢ Keyword cannot be used as variable name, function name or identifiers.
- ➢ Keywords are Case sensitive.
- ➢ 33 keywords exist in Python.

Table 2.1 *Python keywords*

False	elif	lambda
None	else	nonlocal
True	except	not
and	finally	or
as	for	pass
assert	from	raise
break	global	return
class	if	try
continue	import	while
def	in	with
del	is	yield

The following code lists the keywords in Python.

import keyword

```
print(keyword.kwlist)
```

The following code prints the number of keywords in Python i.e. 33.

```
print(len(keyword.kwlist))
```

2.2 IDENTIFIERS

> Identifiers are names given to entities like class, functions, variables etc.
> It helps in differentiating one entity from another.

Rules for identifiers
1. Identifiers can be combination of letters in lowercase(a to z) or uppercase (A to Z) or digits(0 to 9) or an underscore(_)
2. An identifier cannot start with a digit.
3. Keywords cannot be used as identifiers.
4. We cannot use special symbols like !,@,#,$,% etc. as identifiers

TABLE 2.2 *Examples of identifiers*

IDENTIFIERS	VALIDITY	REMARK
Num_1=23	Valid	Satisfies rule 1,2,4
1_num=23	Not valid	Does not satisfy rule 2
Num_1_mark=45	Valid	Satisfies rule 1,2,4
lambda=2	Not valid	Does not satisfy rule 3

mark@= 23	Not valid	Does not satisfy rule 4

2.3 COMMENTS

- ➢ Comments are ignored by compilers or interpreters.
- ➢ It makes code more readable.
- ➢ # symbol is used to write the comment.

TABLE 2.3 *Examples of comments*

SYMBOL	PURPOSE	EXAMPLE
#	Single line comment	#test statement
"""	Multiline comments	"""This is a sample program for Calculating the simple interest"""
'''	Multiline comments	'''This is a sample program for Calculating the simple interest'''

2.4 INDENTATION

- ➢ To define a block of code we use indentation.
- ➢ A code block starts with the indentation and ends with the first unindented line.
- ➢ The amount of indentation is left to the programmer and it must be consistent throughout the block.

> ➤ Generally 4 whitespaces are used for indentation and is preferred over tabs.

Examples 2.1 and 2.2 show the need for indentation in a for loop.

Example 2.1:

Program

```
for i in range(5):

    print(i)
```

Output

0

1

2

3

4

Example 2.2:

Program

```
for i in range(5):

print(i)
```

Output

IndentationError

2.5 STATEMENTS

➢ Instructions that python interpreter can execute are called statements.
➢ Single line statement
> Num=10
➢ Multiline statement – use line continuation character or parenthesis.

Using line continuation character: Num=10+20+\

14+16

Using parenthesis   : Num=(10+20+

14+16)

➢ Multiple statements can exist on a single line for brevity.

a=10;b=20;c=30

2.6 VARIABLES

➢ Variable is a location in memory used to store some data(value).
➢ They are given unique names
➢ Rules for mentioning variable name are same as identifiers.
➢ In Python, there is no need to declare a variable before using it. This is handled internally.

TABLE 2.4 *Examples of variable assignment*

TYPES OF ASSIGNING VALUE TO VARIABLES	EXAMPLES
Single assignment	num=10 height=5.5

	name="raj" num=1+2j
Multiple assignment	num1=num2=num3=10 num,height,name=10,5.5,"raj"

2.7 STORAGE LOCATIONS

➢ Displays address of variable

Example 2.3:

Program

num=10

print(id(num)) #prints the memory location of variable num

Output

1907846496

3. Datatypes

3.1 INTRODUCTION

➢ Every value in python has a datatype.
➢ Since everything in python is an object, data types are actually classes, and variables are instances (objects) of these classes.

3.2 BASIC DATATYPES

➢ Numbers
➢ Boolean
➢ Strings
➢ List
➢ Tuple
➢ Set
➢ Dictionary

3.3 NUMBERS

➢ Integers, floating point numbers, and complex numbers fall under this category. They are defined as int, float and complex classes in python.
➢ type() can be used to know the class of the variable
➢ isinstance() is used to check if the object belongs to a particular class.

Example 3.1

type(num)   #returns the data type of variable num

isinstance(num,int)   #returns true if variable num is an integer

3.4 BOOLEAN:

➢ Represents truth values-True/False

Example 3.2

Program

pass_stud = True

print(type(pass_stud))

Output

<class 'bool'>

3.5 STRINGS

➢ Sequence of Unicode characters (letters, numbers, and special characters).
➢ Single quotes or double quotes are used to represent strings.
➢ Multiline strings can be represented using """or ''' similar to comments.
➢ Strings can be indexed
➢ Strings are immutable.

Example 3.3 shows the two methods for initialisation of strings. Table 3.1 shows the results of various statements when executed on the initialised string.

Example 3.3

Program

str="hello world"

str='hello world'

TABLE 3.1 *Statement,output,explanations of basic string operations*

STATEMENT	OUTPUT	EXPLANATION
print(str[0])	h	prints first character
print(str[-2])	l	prints second character from last
print(str[len(str)-1])	d	prints last character
print(str[6:])	world	performs slicing (slice and print every character from index 6 to end of the string)
print(str[6:9])	wor	performs slicing (slice and print every character from index 6 to index 8)
str[2]="s"	Error	String is immutable
del str	-	deletes the entire string. we cannot delete elements in the string.

3.5.1 CONCATENATION

Example 3.4

Program

string1="Hello"

```
string2="world"

print(string1 + string2)
```

Output

```
Helloworld
```

3.5.2 REPEATING STRINGS

Example 3.5

Program

```
string1="Hello"

string2="world"

Print(string1*3)
```

Output

```
HelloHelloHello
```

3.5.3 ITERATING THROUGH STRING

Example 3.6

Program

```
string1="Hello"

count=0

for i in string1:        #loops through string

    if i=="H":

        count+=1
```

```
print(count)
```

Output

1

3.5.4 MEMBERSHIP TEST

Example 3.7

Program

```
string1="Hello"

print("e" in string1)
```

Output

True

Example 3.8

Program

```
string1="Hello"

print("el" in string1)
```

Output

True

3.5.5 STRING METHODS

- ➢ lower(), upper(), join(), split(), find(), replace(),reverse() etc...

Example 3.9 shows the initialisation of a string. Table 3.2 shows the results of various statements when executed on the initialised string.

Example 3.9

Program

string1="Hello World"

TABLE 3.2 *Statement,output,explanations of various string operations*

STATEMENTS	OUTPUT	EXPLANATION
print(string1.lower())	hello world	Converts the string to lowercase
print(string1.upper())	HELLO WORLD	Converts the string to uppercase
print(string1.split())	['Hello', 'World']	Splits the string at space
print(string1.find("el"))	1	Finds the substring and returns the index
print(string1.replace("Hello", "Hai"))	Hai World	Replaces Hello with Hai but string1 will hold Hello World only as strings are immutable

Example 3.10

Program

```
print(",".join(["Welcome", "to", "the", "course", "of",
"python"]))
```

Output

Welcome,to,the,course,of,python

Example 3.11

Program

```
print(" ".join(["Welcome", "to", "the", "course", "of",
"python"]))
```

Output

Welcome to the course of python

Example 3.12

Program

```
string1="Hello World"

string2=reversed(string1)

print(list(string2))
```

Output

['d', 'l', 'r', 'o', 'W', ' ', 'o', 'l', 'l', 'e', 'H']

Example 3.13

Program

```
string1="Hello"

string2="Hello"
```

```
if (list(string1)==list(string2)):

    print("true")
```

Output

true

3.6 LIST

➢ List is ordered and indexed sequence of items(strings, integers and lsits)
➢ Items need not be of same type.
➢ Items are separated by commas, and are enclosed within square brackets[ ].
➢ List is mutable (values of elements in a list can be changed) data type.

3.6.1 CREATION OF LIST AND INDEXING

Example 3.14

Program

```
stud=[1,23,"raj"]

print(stud[2])
```

Output

raj

3.6.2 LIST OF LISTS

Example 3.15

Program

list1=[[1,23,"raj"],[2,34,"ravi"],[3,54,"raghu"]]

print(list1[1])

Output

[2, 34, 'ravi']

Example 3.16

Program

list1=[[1,23,"raj"],[2,34,"ravi"],[3,54,"raghu"]]

print(len(list1))

Output

3

3.6.3 APPENDING THE LIST

Example 3.17

Program

list1=[[1,23,"raj"],[2,34,"ravi"],[3,54,"raghu"]]

list1.append([4,65,"raju"])

print(list1)

Output

[[1, 23, 'raj'], [2, 34, 'ravi'], [3, 54, 'raghu'], [4, 65, 'raju']]

Example 3.18

Program

```
list1=[1,2,3,4]

list2=[5,6,7,8]

new_list=list1+list2

print(new_list)
```

Output

```
[1, 2, 3, 4, 5, 6, 7, 8]
```

3.6.4 INSERTING IN THE LIST

Example 3.19

Program

```
list1=[1,2,4]

list1.insert(2,3)                    #inserting at position 2

print(list1)
```

Output

```
[1, 2, 3, 4]
```

3.6.5 DELETING THE LIST ELEMENTS

Example 3.20

Program

```
list1=[1,2,3,4]

del list1[1]

print(list1)
```

Output

[1, 3, 4]

Example 3.21

Program

list1=[1,2,3,4]

list1.pop(1)

print(list1)

Output

[1, 3, 4]

Example 3.22

Program

list1=["apple", "mango", "jack"]

list1.remove("apple")

print(list1)

Output

['mango', 'jack']

3.6.6 CHECK LIST ELEMENTS

Example 3.23

Program

list1=["apple", "mango", "jack"]

```
if("apple" in list1):

    print("element present")
```

Output

element present

Example 3.24

Program

```
list1=["apple", "mango", "jack"]

if("banana" not in list1):

    print("element not present")
```

Output

element not present

3.6.7 **LIST REVERSING**

Example 3.25

Program

```
list1=["apple", "mango", "jack"]

list1.reverse()

print(list1)
```

Output

['jack', 'mango', 'apple']

3.6.8 **SORTING THE LIST**

Example 3.26 shows the initialisation and sorting of a list. Table 3.3 shows the results of various statements when executed on the sorted list.

Example 3.26

Program

list1=[11,72,33,24]

sort_list=sorted(list1)

TABLE 3.3 *Statement,output,explanations of various string operations*

STATEMENTS	OUTPUT	EXPLANATION
print(sort_list)	[11, 24, 33, 72]	Prints the sorted list
print(sorted(list1,reverse=True))	[72, 33, 24, 11]	Prints the sorted list in reverse order
print(sorted(list1))	[11, 24, 33, 72]	Prints the sorted list
list1.sort() print(list1)	[11, 24, 33, 72]	Sorts and stores in list1 itself

3.6.9 REFERENCES IN LIST

Example 3.27

Program
list1=["apple", "mango", "jack"]

list_ref=list1

list_ref.append("banana")

print(list1)

Output

['apple', 'mango', 'jack', 'banana']

3.6.10 **SPLITTING IN LIST**

Example 3.28

Program

list1="This is a sample program"

ls=list1.split()

print(ls)

Output

['This', 'is', 'a', '', 'sample', 'program']

Example 3.29

Program

list1="10,20,30,40"

ls=list1.split(",")

print(ls)

Output

['10', '20', '30', '40']

3.6.11 **INDEXING IN THE LIST**

Example 3.30

Program

list1=[1,2,3,4]

print(list1[1])

#prints the second element as index starts at 0

Output

2

Example 3.31

Program

list1=[1,2,3,4]

print(list1[-1])   # prints last element in the list

Output

4

Example 3.32

Program

list1=[1,2,3,4]

print(list1[-2])

#prints the second last element in the list

Output

3

3.6.12 LIST SLICING

➢ Used for accessing segments of the list

Example 3.33 shows the initialisation of a list. Table 3.4 shows the results of various slicing statements when executed on the list.

Example 3.33

Program

list1=[1,2,3,4]

TABLE 3.4 *Statement,output,explanations of various slice operations*

STATEMENT	OUTPUT	EXPLANATION
print(list1[:])	[1, 2, 3, 4]	prints all elements
print(list1[0:3])	[1, 2, 3]	prints from 1st element to 3rd element in the list
print(list1[::2])	[1, 3]	prints alternate elements(as step size is 2)
print(list1[1::2])	[2, 4]	prints alternate elements starting from index 1

3.6.13 COUNTING THE LIST ELEMENTS

Example 3.34

Program

list1=[1,1,2,3,4]

print(list1.count(1))

Output

2   (since 1 occurs 2 times output is 2)

3.6.14 **LENGTH OF THE LIST**

Example 3.35

Program

list1=[1,1,2,3,4]

print(len(list1))

Output

5

3.6.15 **LIST LOOPING**

Example 3.36

Program

list1=[1,1,2,3,4]

for num in list1:

    print(num)

Output

1 1 2 3 4

3.6.16 **LIST COMPREHENSION**

Example 3.37

Program

```
list1=[i*2 for i in range(10)]
print(list1)
```

Output

[0, 2, 4, 6, 8, 10, 12, 14, 16, 18]

Example 3.38

Program

```
list1=[1,2,3,4]
list2=[i*2 for i in list1]
print(list2)
```

Output

[2, 4, 6, 8]

Example 3.39

Program

```
list1=[1,2,3,4]
list2=[i*2 for i in list1 if i>2]
print(list2)
```

Output

[6, 8]

Example 3.40

> **Program**
>
> list1=[1,2,3,4]
>
> list2=[(i,i*2) for i in list1 if i>2]
>
> print(list2)
>
> **Output**
>
> [(3, 6), (4, 8)]

3.6.17 MATRIX OPERATIONS (TRANSPOSE)

Example 3.40

> **Program**
>
> matrix_a=[[1,2],[3,4],[5,6]]
>
> transpose_mat=[[row[i] for row in matrix_a] for i in range(2)]
>
> print(transpose_mat)
>
> **Output**
>
> [[1, 3, 5], [2, 4, 6]]

3.7 TUPLE

> ➢ Tuple is ordered sequence of items and the items need not be of same type.

➢ Items are separated by commas, and are enclosed within parenthesis( ).

➢ Tuple is immutable (values of elements in a list cannot be changed) data type.

Various ways of creating a tuple are as follows.

stud=(1,23,"raj")

stud=(1,(2,3),(3,4))   #nested tuple

stud=(1,(2,3),[3,4])   # creating a list in tuple

Example 3.41 shows the initialisation of a tuple. Table 3.5 shows the results of various operations executed on the tuple.

Example 3.41

Program

stud=(1,23,"raj")

TABLE 3.5 *Statement,output,explanations of various tuple operations*

STATEMENT	OUTPUT	EXPLANATION
stud[1]=25	Error	Error as tuple is immutable
print(len(stud))	3	Prints length of tuple
print(stud.index(1))	0	prints the index of element 1
print(1 in stud)	True	prints True if 1 is present in the tuple(membership function)

| print(stud[1]) | 23 | prints tuple element at index position 1 |
| print(stud[-1]) | raj | prints last element in tuple |

Example 3.42 shows the initialisation of a tuple. Table 3.6 shows the results of various operations executed on nested tuple.

Example 3.42

    Program

    stud=(1,23,("raj","ravi"))

TABLE 3.6 *Statement,output,explanations of various nested tuple operations*

STATEMENT	OUTPUT	EXPLANATION
print(stud[-1])	('raj', 'ravi')	prints last element in tuple
print(stud[-1][1])	ravi	prints the last element in the embedded tuple

Example 3.43 shows the initialisation of a tuple. Table 3.7 shows the results of various operations executed on nested tuple.

Example 3.43

    Program

    stud=(10,20,30,40)

TABLE 3.7 *Statement,output,explanations of various tuple methods*

STATEMENT	OUTPUT	EXPLANATION
print(stud[1:3])	(20, 30)	Slicing operation(slices 2nd and 3rd elements)
print(stud[1:-2])	(20,)	prints the slice from 2nd element upto 3rd last element
print(min(stud))	10	prints minimum element in tuple
print(max(stud))	40	prints maximum element in tuple
print(sum(stud))	100	prints the sum of all elements in the tuple

Example 3.44

Program

stud=(1,(2,3),[3,4])

stud[2][1]=5

print(stud)

Output

(1, (2, 3), [3, 5])   #tuple is immutable but list is mutable

3.7.1 CONCATENATING TUPLES

Example 3.45

Program

stud1=(10,20,30,40)

stud2=(50,60,70)

print(stud1+stud2)

Output

(10, 20, 30, 40, 50, 60, 70)

3.7.2 REPEATING THE TUPLE

Example 3.46

Program

stud1=(10,20,30,40)

print(stud1*4)

Output

(10, 20, 30, 40, 10, 20, 30, 40, 10, 20, 30, 40, 10, 20, 30, 40)

3.7.3 DELETING A TUPLE

del stud

3.7.4 COUNTING THE ELEMENTS IN TUPLE

Example 3.47

Program

```
stud=(10,20,30,10)
print(stud.count(10))   #prints the count of 10 in the tuple
```

Output

2

3.7.5 SORTING A TUPLE

Example 3.48

Program

```
stud=(10,20,30,15)
stud1=sorted(stud)
print(stud1)
```

Output

[10, 15, 20, 30]

3.8 SET

- ➤ Set is an unordered, mutable collection of unique items.
- ➤ Set is defined by values separated by commas inside braces {}.
- ➤ Set operations like union, intersection, can be performed on two sets.

Example 3.49

Program

marks={10,20,30}

print(marks[1])

Output

Error   #since it is unordered collection of items

Example 3.50

Program

marks={10,10,20,30}

print(marks)

Output

{10, 20, 30}   #since no duplicates allowed

3.8.1 ADD ELEMENT

Example 3.51

Program

marks={10,20,30}

marks.add(40)

print(marks)

Output

{40, 10, 20, 30}

Example 3.52

Program

```
marks={40,10,20,30}

marks.update([60,15])

print(marks)
```

Output

{40, 10, 15, 20, 60, 30}

3.8.2 REMOVE ELEMENT

Example 3.53

Program

```
marks={10,20,30}

marks.discard(20)

print(marks)
```

Output

{10, 30}

Example 3.54

Program

```
marks={10,20,30}

marks.remove(30)
```

print(marks)

Output

{10, 20}

Example 3.55

Program

marks={10,20,30}

print(marks.pop())

Output

10

Example 3.56

Program

marks={10,20,30}

marks.clear()

print(marks)

Output

set()

3.8.3 SET OPERATIONS

3.8.3.1 UNION

Example 3.57

Program

mark1={10,20,30}

mark2={30,40,50}

mark=mark1|mark2   #union operation

print(mark)

Output

{50, 20, 40, 10, 30}

Example 3.58

Program

mark1={10,20,30}

mark2={30,40,50}

mark=mark1.union(mark2)

print(mark)

Output

{50, 20, 40, 10, 30}

3.8.3.2 INTERSECTION (ELEMENTS THAT ARE PRESENT BOTH IN SET1 AND SET2)

Example 3.59

Program

mark1={10,20,30}

mark2={30,40,50}

```
mark=mark1&mark2   #intersection operation
```

```
print(mark)
```

Output

```
{30}
```

Example 3.60

Program

```
mark1={10,20,30}
```

```
mark2={30,40,50}
```

```
mark=mark1.intersection(mark2)
```

```
print(mark)
```

Output

```
{30}
```

3.8.3.3 DIFFERENCE (ELEMENTS THAT ARE PRESENT IN SET1 AND NOT IN SET2)

Example 3.61

Program

```
mark1={10,20,30}
```

```
mark2={30,40,50}
```

```
mark=mark1-mark2
```

```
print(mark)
```

Output

{10, 20}

Example 3.62

Program

```
mark1={10,20,30}

mark2={30,40,50}

mark=mark1.difference(mark2)

print(mark)
```

Output

{10, 20}

3.8.3.4 SYMMETRIC DIFFERENCE (ELEMENTS IN BOTH SETS LEAVING THE ELEMENTS THAT ARE COMMON)

Example 3.63

Program

```
mark1={10,20,30}

mark2={30,40,50}

mark=mark1^mark2 #symmetric difference operation

print(mark)
```

Output

{40, 10, 50, 20}

Example 3.64

Program

mark1={10,20,30}

mark2={30,40,50}

mark=mark1.symmetric_difference(mark2)

print(mark)

Output:

{40, 10, 50, 20}

3.8.3.5 SUBSET

Example 3.65

Program

mark1={10,20,30}

mark2={10}

print(mark2.issubset(mark1))

Output

True

3.8.3.6 FROZEN SETS(IMMUTABLE SETS)

➢ Frozen sets are hashable and can be used as keys to dictionary.
➢ Frozen set supports union, intersection, difference, symmetric difference.

➢ Frozen sets being immutable we cannot add or delete elements.

Example 3.66

Program

mark1=frozenset([10,20,30,40])

print(mark1)

Output

frozenset({40, 10, 20, 30})

3.9 DICTIONARY

➢ Dictionary is an unordered collection of key-value pairs.
➢ Defined by {} with each item being a pair in the form of key:value.

Example 3.67

Program

dict={"name":"raj", "age":"34"}

print(dict["name"])

Output

raj

Example 3.68

Program

```
dict={1:"apple",2:"mango"}
```

```
print(dict[1])
```

Output

apple

Example 3.69

Program

```
dict={1:"apple","size":"big"}
```

```
print(dict["size"])
```

Output

big

Example 3.70

Program

```
dict={}.fromkeys(["apple","mango"],0)
```

```
#assigns key 0 to the values in the dictionary
```

```
print(dict)
```

Output

{'apple': 0, 'mango': 0}

3.9.1 ACCESSING THE DICTIONARY

Example 3.71 shows the initialisation of a dictionary. Table 3.8 shows the results of various operations executed on the dictionary.

Example 3.71

Program

dict={1:"apple",2:"mango"}

TABLE 3.8 *Statement,output,explanations of various dictionary methods*

STATEMENT	OUTPUT	EXPLANATION
print(dict.items())	dict_items([(1, 'apple'), (2, 'mango')])	Prints the items in the dictionary
print(dict.keys())	dict_keys([1, 2])	Prints the keys in the dictionary
print(dict.values())	dict_values(['apple', 'mango'])	Prints the values in the dictionary
for i in dict.items(): print(i)	(1, 'apple') (2, 'mango')	Parses the dictionary items and prints the key-value pairs

3.9.2 ADD OR MODIFY ELEMENTS IN DICTIONARY

Example 3.72

Program

dict={1:"apple",2: "mango"}

dict[1]="jack fruit"

print(dict[1])

Output

jack fruit

Example 3.73

Program

```
dict={1:"apple",2: "mango"}

dict[3]="jack fruit"

print(dict)
```

Output

{1: 'apple', 2: 'mango', 3: 'jack fruit'}

3.9.3 DELETE OR REMOVE ELEMENT

Example 3.74

Program

```
dict={1:"apple",2: "mango"}

dict.popitem()

print(dict)
```

Output

{1: 'apple'}

Example 3.75

Program

```
dict={1:"apple",2: "mango"}

dict.pop(1)
```

```
print(dict)
```

Output

```
{2: 'mango'}
```

Example 3.76

Program

```
dict={1:"apple",2: "mango"}

del dict[1]

print(dict)
```

Output

```
{2: 'mango'}
```

Example 3.77

Program

```
dict={1:"apple",2: "mango"}

dict.clear()

print(dict)
```

Output

```
{}
```

3.9.4 COPYING THE DICTIONARY

Example 3.78

Program

dict={1:"apple",2: "mango"}

dict_copy= dict.copy()

print(dict_copy)

Output

{1: 'apple', 2: 'mango'}

Example 3.79

Program

dict={1:"apple",2:"mango"}

#copies all items in dictionary except value ='mango'

dict_copy={k:v for k,v in dict.items() if v!="mango"}

print(dict_copy)

Output

{1: 'apple'}

3.10 CONVERSION BETWEEN DATATYPES

➢ Convert data type by using data type conversion functions like int(),float(),str() etc.

1. float(5)   converts integer 5 to 5.0

2. marks=[10,20,30]

   m=set(marks) -converts list to set data type

3. list("raj") -converts string to list

4.Input and Output Operations

4.1 OUTPUT OPERATIONS

1. print("hello world")   #output: "hello world"

2. a="how are you"

   print("hai "+a)   #output: hai how are you

3. a=2019

   print("happy new year", a)   #output: happy new year 2019

4. a="hai"; b="welcome"

   print("{} I {} you all to this gathering".format(a,b))

   #output: hai I welcome you all to this gathering

   1. print("Hai {name}, Welcome to
      {country}".format(name="Raj",country="India"))
      #output: Hai Raj, Welcome to India
   2. print("Hai {0}, Welcome to
      {country}".format("Raj",country="India"))
      #output: Hai Raj, Welcome to India

4.2 INPUT OPERATIONS

1. mark=input("Enter your mark")

A dialog box appears and the data entered will be assigned to variable mark. The value assigned to mark will be a string.

2. mark=int(input("Enter your mark"))

The value assigned to variable mark will be an integer as the input statement is prefixed with int().

3. Taking multiple inputs in python is possible using split() function.

Example 4.1

Program

```
x, y = input("Enter  two values: ").split()

print("the value of x is ",x)

print("the value of y is ", y)
```

Output

```
Enter two values: 23 34

# two values should be given by user with " " as separator

the value of x is  23

the value of y is  34
```

Example 4.2

Program

```
m,n=[int(x) for x in input().split(",")]

print("m value ",m)

print("n value", n)
```

Output

12,34   #input is given with ',' as separator

m value 12

n value 34

Example 4.3

Program

a=[int(x) for x in input().split()]

print(a)

Output

12 32 45 56   #multiple inputs given with " " as separator

[12, 32, 45, 56]   #output is a list

5.Operators

Operators are special symbols that are used in performing computations.

Various types of operators are

1. Arithmetic operators
2. Relational operators
3. Boolean operators
4. Bitwise operators
5. Assignment operators
6. Special operators

5.1 ARITHMETIC OPERATORS

Various arithmetic operators are   +(Addition),-(Subtraction), *(Multiplication), /(Division), %(Modulo Division), // (Floor division) and ** (Exponent)

Example 5.1 shows the initialisation of 2 variables. Table 5.1 shows the results of various arithmetic operations executed on the variables.

Example 5.1

Program

a=10; b=20

TABLE 5.1 *Statement, output and explanation of various arithmetic operations*

STATEMENT	OUTPUT	EXPLANATION
print(a+b)	30	Addition operation
print(a-b)	-10	Subtraction operation
print(a*b)	200	Multiplication operation
print(a/b)	0.5	Division operation
print(a//b)	0	Floor division
print(a**b)	100000000000000000000	Exponentiation

5.2 RELATIONAL OPERATORS

<, >, ==, !=, >=, <= are comparison(relational) operators.

Example 5.2 shows the initialisation of 2 variables. Table 5.2 shows the results of various relational operations executed on the variables.

Example 5.2

Program

a=10; b=20

TABLE 5.2 *Statement, output and explanation of various relational operations*

STATEMENT	OUTPUT	EXPLANATION
print(a<b)	True	Less than operation
print(a>b)	False	Greater than operation
print(a==b)	False	Equal to operation

5.3 LOGICAL OPERATORS

and, or and not are logical operators.

Example 5.3

Program

a= True; b=False

print(a and b)   # 'and 'operation

Output

False

5.4 BITWISE OPERATORS

Bitwise operators are &(AND) , |(OR), ~(NOT), ^(XOR), >>(Right shift) and <<(Left shift)

Example 5.4

Program

a=10; b=5

print(a & b)   # bitwise AND operations

print(a | b)   #bitwise OR operation

Output

0

15

5.5 ASSIGNMENT OPERATORS

Various assignment operators are =, +=, -=, *=, /=, %=, //=, **=, &=, |=, ^=, >>= and <<=

Example 5.5

Program

a=10

a+=10   # add and assignment operations

print(a)

Output

20

Similarly we can perform various operations using other assignment operators.

5.6 SPECIAL OPERATORS

5.6.1 IDENTITY OPERATORS

➤ is and is not are identity operators.
➤ They are used to check if two variables are in same part of the memory.

Example 5.6

Program

a=10; b=10

print(a is b)

Output

True

Example 5.7

Program

a=10; b=15

print(a is b)

Output

False

Example 5.8

Program

a=10; b=15

print(a is not b)

Output

True

Example 5.9

Program

list1=[1,2,3]

list2=[1,2,3]

print(list1 is list2)

Output

False

5.6.2 MEMBERSHIP OPERATORS

➢ in and not in are membership operators.
➢ They are used to find whether a value or variable is present in a sequence(string, dictionary, tuple set or list)

Example 5.10

Program

list1=[1,2,3]

print(1 in list1)

Output

True

Example 5.11

Program

dict1={1:"apple",2:"mango"}

print(1 in dict1)   #will check only keys

Output

True

6. Decision Making and Branching

➢ If, elif, else statements are conditional statements

➢ They are used in decision making

Example 6.1

Program

```
a=15

if(a%2 == 0):

    print("a is even number")

else:

    print("a is odd number")
```

Output

a is odd number

Example 6.2

Program

```
a=16

if(a%2 == 0):

    print("a is even number")

elif(a%2 ==1):

    print("a is odd number")
```

Output

a is even number

Example 6.3: Nested if

Program

```
a=16; b=14
if(a%2 == 0):
    if(b%2==0):
        print("a and b are even numbers")
    else:
        print("a is even number")
```

Output

a and b are even numbers

Example 6.4

Program

```
a=16; b=14
if(a%2 == 0 and b%2==0):
    print("a and b are even numbers")
```

Output

a and b are even numbers

Note: 0 and None are considered as false. Everything else is considered as True.

7. Decision Making and Looping

While and *for* are looping statements in Python.

7.1 WHILE STATEMENT

Syntax

while expression:

> body of while

Example 7.1

> **Program**
>
> a=5; i=0
>
> while (i<a):
>
>> print(i)
>>
>> i=i+1
>
> **Output**
>
> 0
>
> 1
>
> 2
>
> 3
>
> 4

Example 7.2

Program

a=5; i=0

while (i<a):

    print(i)

    i=i+1

else:

    print("index greater than length of a")

Output

0

1

2

3

4

index greater than length of a

7.2 FOR STATEMENT

For loop in python is used to iterate over a sequence (list, tuple, string) or other iterate-able objects.

Syntax:

for element in sequence:

    body of for

Example 7.3

Program

```
list1=[10,20,30]
for i in list1:
    print(i)
```

Output

```
10
20
30
```

Example 7.4 range() –generates sequence of numbers

Program

```
for i in range(5):
    print(i)
```

Output

```
0
1
2
3
4
```

Example 7.5

Program

```
for i in range(1,10,2):

    print(i)
```

Output

1

3

5

7

9

Example 7.6

Program

```
for i in range(1,10,2):

    print(i)

else:

    print("no more items")
```

Output

```
1
3
5
7
9
no more items
```

7.2.1 **NESTED FOR STATEMENT**

Example 7.7

Program

```
for i in range(1,4,2):

    for j in range(1,5):

        print(i*j)
```

Output

```
1
2
3
4
3
6
9
12
```

7.3 BREAK, CONTINUE STATEMENTS

➢ Break and Continue statements can alter the flow of the looping statements.

Example 7.8

Program

```
for i in range(1,4,2):

    for j in range(1,5):

        if(i==3):

            break

        print(i*j)
```

Output

1
2
3
4

Example 7.9

Program

```python
for i in range(1,4,2):

    for j in range(1,5):

        if(j==3):

            continue

        print(i*j)
```

Output

1
2
4
3
6
12

8. Functions

➢ Functions consists of group of statements that can perform a specific task.

➢ It enables modular programming.

➢ It enables the concept of reusability and enhances readability, understand ability.

➢ Through Parameters (arguments) values are passed to a function.

➢ Return statement returns the value from the function and it is optional. Default return value is None.

8.1 ELEMENTS OF FUNCTION

8.1.1 FUNCTION DEFINITION

Syntax

def function_name(parameters):   #parameters are optional

   Statements   #indented statements

8.1.2 FUNCTION CALL

Syntax

Function_name(parameters)

8.1.3 ACTUAL PARAMETERS AND FORMAL PARAMETERS

➢ The parameters that are in the function call are actual parameters

➢ The parameters that are present in the function definition are formal parameters.

8.1.4 DEFAULT ARGUMENTS

➤ If an argument in the function definition is assigned a default value and if the function call does not pass the value for this argument, the default value will be considered inside the function.

➤ It is better to use default arguments after all non-default arguments in the function definition.

Example 8.1

Program

def add(num,num1=10):#num1 is the default argument

   return num+num1

print(add(5))

#default argument value is not passed to the function

Output

15

8.1.5 KEYWORD ARGUMENTS

➤ Normally, when we call a function with arguments, the values will be assigned to their arguments based on their positions.

➤ But, when we use keyword arguments we can change their positions.

➤ Keyword arguments are also called as named arguments.

➤ The function call will be made with keyworded, variable length argument list with their values.

➤ The argument in the function definition would be ****kwargs.**

➤ kwarg matches the keyword with their values.

➢ So, if variable length arguments are to be passed to a function, keyword arguments are used.

➢ This is widely used in data science applications.

Example 8.2

Program

```
def rank_card(**kwargs):

    print("Your name is {1} and grade is
{0}".format(kwargs["grade"],kwargs["name"]))

    rank_card(name="Ravi",grade="A")
```

Output

Your name is Ravi and grade is A

8.1.6 ARBITRARY ARGUMENTS

➢ When the number of arguments that are to be passed to a function is not known in advance, arbitrary arguments are used.

➢ The argument in the function definition would be **names.**

Example 8.3

Program

```
def rank_card(*names):

  for name in names:

    print("Your name is {0}".format(name))

rank_card("Ravi","Raj", "Reena")
```

Output

Your name is Ravi

Your name is Raj

Your name is Reena

8.1.7 RETURN STATEMENT

Syntax

return(expression_list)

Example 8.4

The function circ_area calculates the area of a circle when the radius is passed as a parameter. The area calculated in the function is returned back using a return statement.

Program

```
import math
def circ_area(rad):    #function definition
    return math.pi*(rad**2)
x=circ_area(5) #function call
print (x)
```

Output

78.53981633974483

8.1.8 SCOPE AND LIFE TIME OF VARIABLES

> Variables defined inside the function have local scope(recognition).
> Life time of those variables (period for which the variables reside in the memory) is the period for which the function executes.

Example 8.5

Program

sum=0

def list_sum(list1):

   total=0

   for num in list1:

     total=total+num

   return total

list_num=[1,2,3,4]

sum=list_sum(list_num)

print(sum)

Output

10

In this example total and num are local variables of function list_sum and the scope of the variables is local to the function. Whereas, the variable sum has global scope and can be accessed outside the function. In order to declare a variable as global we can use the keyword **global (optional).**

8.2 TYPES OF FUNCTIONS

Functions are of 2 types.

1. Built-in functions
2. User-defined functions

8.2.1 BUILT-IN FUNCTIONS

Some widely used built-in functions are explained below.

1. abs()-returns absolute value of a number

Example 8.6

> **Program**
> print(abs(-2.5))
> **Output**
> 2.5

2. all()-returns True if all elements in a list,tuple and set are true

Example 8.7

> **Program**
> list1=[1,2,3,4]
> print(all(list1))
> **Output**
> True

3. divmod()-takes two numbers and returns the quotient and remainder as a tuple.

Example 8.8

> **Program**
> print(divmod(12,3))

Output

(4, 0)

4. enumerate()-returns the index and actual value of an iterable (list,set,tuple)

Example 8.9

Program

```
list1=[1,2,3,4]
for index,num in enumerate(list1):
    print("index is {i} and value is {j}".format(i=index,j=num))
```
Output

index is 0 and value is 1

index is 1 and value is 2

index is 2 and value is 3

index is 3 and value is 4

5. filter()-function that can be used to filter out the values in larger list, tuple and set by applying the function on each element. It returns the new list, tuple and set.

Example 8.10

Program

```
def even(num):
    if(num%2==0):
        return num
list1=[2,3,4,5,6]
list_even=list(filter(even,list1))
#filters the even numbers in the list using function even
print(list_even)
```
Output

[2, 4, 6]

6. isinstance()-checks if the first argument is an instance of second argument which is a class.

Example 8.11

Program
```
list1=[1,2,3,4]
print(isinstance(list1,list))
#checks if list1 is an instance of list class
```
Output
```
True
```
7. map()-applies a function to all items in the list

Example 8.12

Program
```
def exp(num):
    num=num**2
    return num
list1=[2,3,4,5,6]
list_even=list(map(exp,list1))
#applies exp function on all items in the list
print(list_even)
```
Output
```
[4, 9, 16, 25, 36]
```
8. reduce()-performs computations on sequential pairs of values in a list and returns it. It is to be imported from functools module.

Example 8.13

Program
```
from functools import reduce
def add(num,num1):
    return num+num1
list1=[2,3,4,5,6]
list_sum=reduce(add,list1)
#adds consecutive elements in list
print(list_sum)
```

Output

20

map(), reduce() and filter() are widely used in data science application development.

8.2.2 USER DEFINED FUNCTIONS

The function written by the user inorder to perform a particular action is called as user defined function. The function definition, function call, arguments and return statements have been already discussed in section 8.1.

8.3 RECURSIVE FUNCTION

If a function calls itself then it is recursive function. Advantages of recursion are

> ➤ Code is concise
> ➤ Complex tasks can be done by modularisation

Disadvantages are

> ➤ It is hard to understand and hence debugging is difficult.
> ➤ It is expensive in terms of memory usage.

Following example finds the factorial of a number by performing recursion.

Example 8.14

Program

```
def fact(n):

    if n==1:                    #boundary case

        return 1

    else:

        return(n*fact(n-1))     #recursive call

print("Factorial of 5 is ",fact(5))
```

Output

120

8.4 ANONYMOUS AND LAMBDA FUNCTION

➢ Anonymous functions are defined without a name.
➢ Anonymous functions are defined using lambda keyword.
➢ Lambda functions are used with filter(), map() and reduce() built-in functions.

Syntax:

lambda arguments: expression

Example 8.15

Let us first consider a function pow(a,n) that calculates a^n.

Program

```
def power(a,n):

    return(a**n)
```

print(power(2,5))

Output

32

This function can be written using lambda functions as follows.

Example 8.16

Program

power=lambda a,n: a**n

print(power(2,5))

Output

32

We can combine lambda functions with filter() function as follows.

Example 8.17

Program

list1=[2,3,4,5,6]

list_even=list(filter(lambda x:(x%2==0),list1))

#filters the even numbers in the list

print(list_even)

Output:

[2, 4, 6]

We can combine lambda function with map() in-built function as follows.

Example 8.18

Program

```
list1=[2,3,4,5,6]

list_even=list(map(lambda x:(x**2),list1))

#finds the power of 2 for each element in the list

print(list_even)
```

Output

[4, 9, 16, 25, 36]

We can combine lambda function with reduce() in-built function as follows.

Example 8.19

Program

```
from functools import reduce

list1=[2,3,4,5,6]

#finds the sum of consecutive elements in the list

list_even=reduce(lambda x,y:(x+y),list1)

print(list_even)
```

Output

20

From the above examples we can understand that by using lambda functions we can write the code more elegantly and concisely.

9. Modules and Packages

9.1 MODULES

> ➤ Module is a file containing python statements and definitions.
> ➤ Any file stored with .py extension is a module.
> ➤ We can import the modules using import statement.

For instance, if there exists a file add.py then we can import this file by writing

import add

Similarly, there are many mathematical functions stored in math file which can be imported.

Example 9.1

Program

import math

print(math.sqrt(12))

Output

3.4641016151377544

We can do the above calculation using an alias as shown below.

Example 9.2

Program

import math as m

```
print(m.sqrt(12))
```

Output

3.4641016151377544

We can also import specific names from a module instead of importing the whole module as shown below.

```
from datetime import datetime
```

```
from math import ceil
```

The following example shows how module written by a user can be imported in another module.

Example 9.3

Program

```
import math
```

```
def circ_area(rad):
```

```
    return math.pi*(rad**2)
```

The above statements that calculates the area of a circle are stored in circ.py. This module can be imported in another file as follows.

Example 9.3.1

Program

```
import circ
```

```
radius=3
```

```
area=circ_area(radius)
```

print(area)

Output:

28.274333882308138

9.2 PACKAGES

- ➢ Packages help in organising python's modules as a directory structure.
- ➢ Packages contain sub-packages and modules themselves.
- ➢ A package should have __init__.py file in it.
- ➢ __init__.py file can be empty, and it indicates that the directory it contains is a Python package.
- ➢ The initialisation code for the package is normally placed in the __init__.py file.
- ➢ Packages can be imported the same way a module is imported.

The following statement shows the method to import a package.

import sound.effects.echo

In the above example sound is a package, effects is a sub-package and echo is a module.

10. File Handling

Files are used to store the data permanently in non-volatile memory.

Various file operations are

1. Opening a file
2. Closing a file
3. Reading from a file
4. Writing to a file
5. Renaming a file
6. Deleting a file

10.1 OPEN A FILE

The command that is used to open the file is

fp=open("example.txt")

#opens file in current directory

File can be opened in different modes. Different modes and their description are explained in Table 10.1.

TABLE 10.1 *File opening modes and their descriptions*

Mode	Description
'r'	Opens file for reading(default)
'w'	Opens file for writing. If file does not exist, it creates a new file.

	If file exists it truncates the file.
'x'	Creates a new file. If file already exists, the operation fails.
'a'	Opens file in append mode. If file does not exist, it creates a new file.
't'	This is the default mode. It opens in text mode.
'b'	This opens in binary mode.
'+'	This will open a file for reading and writing (updating)

Files can be opened in different modes as shown below.

```
fp=open("example.txt",'w')      #opens a file for writing

fp=open("example.txt",'r')    #opens a file for reading

fp=open("example.txt",encoding='utf-8')

#choosing the encoding format
```

10.2 CLOSE A FILE

The command that is used to close the file is

```
fp.close()
```

It is always safe to put the file close statement in try, except, finally block. This will be discussed in next chapter.

10.3 READ FROM A FILE

Various read operation commands are listed below.

fp.read()

reads the entire file starting from the current cursor position

fp.read(4)

#reads the next 4 characters from the current cursor position

fp.seek(0)   #moves the cursor to start of the file

fp.tell()   #returns the current cursor position

fp.readline()   #returns the individual lines in the file

10.4 WRITE TO A FILE

The following command will write the string in the file pointed by the file pointer fp.

fp.write("Welcome to file handling")

fp.close()   #it is always better to close the file after writing

10.5 RENAMING FILE

The following set of commands will rename the file *example.txt* as *sample.txt*. It is necessary to import os package for accomplishing this.

import os

os.rename("example.txt","sample.txt")

10.6 DELETING A FILE

The following set of commands will remove the file *example.txt*. It is necessary to import os package for accomplishing this.

```
import os
```

```
os.remove("example.txt")
```

11. Exception Handling and Debugging

➤ Errors that occur due improper syntax results in syntax error.
➤ Errors in programming logic results in logical errors.
➤ Errors that can occur at runtime are called exceptions.

For example, FileNotFoundError, ZeroDivisionError are exceptions raised by the interpreters.

To avoid the exceptions they are to be handled as shown below.

11.1 EXCEPTION HANDLING

Example 11.1

Program

```
a=4
b=0
try:
    print(a/b)
except:
    print("zero division")
```

Output

zero division

By writing the exception handling statements the exceptions will be handled properly. In the above example, ZeroDivisionError is handled. More than 1 except blocks can be present while handling the exceptions.

11.2 RAISE EXCEPTIONS

If the user wants to raise an error, exceptions can be raised as follows..

raise KeyboardInterrupt

Example 11.2

Program

```
try:
    number=int(input("Enter a number greater than 10"))
    if number<=10:
        raise ValueError("Error")
    except ValueError as err:
        print(err)
```

Output

3   #input given

Error

Prints "Error" if the input given is less than or equal to 10.

11.3 TRY..FINALLY

➤ Finally clause is optional in Python.
➤ It is written at the end of the try block.
➤ This block is executed always.

Example 11.3

Program

a=4

b=0

try:

   print(a/b)

except:

   print("zero division")

finally:

   print("program ends")

Output

zero division

program ends

11.4 DEBUGGING IN PYTHON

Debugging in Python can be done using pdb (Python debugger) statement. The following program tells the use of pdb.

Example 11.4

Program

```
import pdb

i=0

for i in range(10):

    print(i)

    pdb.set_trace()
```

In the above program, every time when "i" is incremented the set trace function will be called and a dialog box will appear.

Some important characters that can be given in the dialog box and their functionalities are listed below.

c: continue→ continues the execution till the next time pdb statement is executed

p: print → prints the value of the given variable

q: quit→ quits the debugger

h: help→ prints all the debugger functions that can be used

list →tells the position of the execution

p locals()→ prints all local variable values

p globals()→ prints all global variable values

For instance, in the above example if

p i

is given in the dialog box the value of i will be printed.

12. Pyplot

Matplotlib.pyplot is a plotting library for python programming language. Pyplot functions can create a plotting area, plot lines, create plot labels etc.

Sample code is given below.

Example 12.1

Program

```
import matplotlib.pyplot as plt

plt.plot([1,2,3,4])        #y axis values

plt.xlabel('Indices')

plt.ylabel('Numbers')

plt.title('Plot Exercise')

plt.show()                 # x axis values will start from 0
```

Output

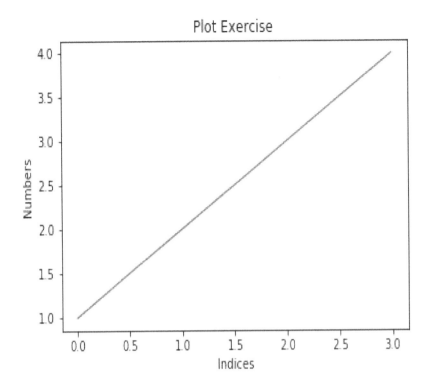

Example 12.2

Program

```
import matplotlib.pyplot as plt

plt.plot([1,2,3,4],[2,4,6,8])     # x and y axis values

plt.xlabel('Indices')

plt.ylabel('Numbers')

plt.title('Plot Exercise')

plt.grid()                        #grid is on

plt.show()
```

Output

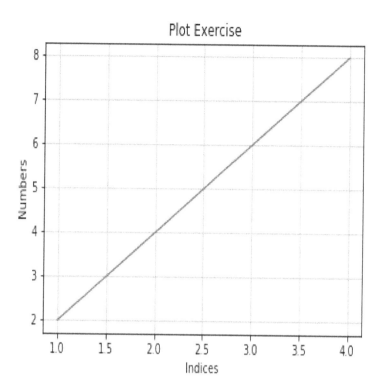

Example 12.3

Program

```
import matplotlib.pyplot as plt

plt.plot([1,2,3,4],[2,4,6,8],'ro')

#points are plotted as red dots

plt.xlabel('Indices')

plt.ylabel('Numbers')

plt.title('Plot Exercise')
```

plt.show()

Output

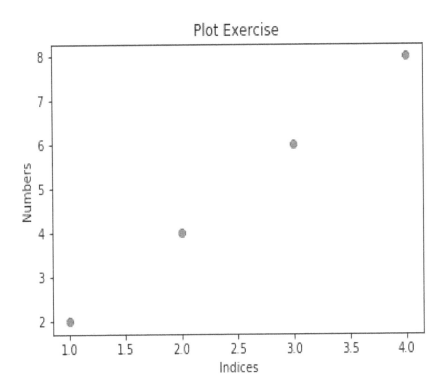

Example 12.4

Program

import matplotlib.pyplot as plt

import numpy as np

x=np.arange(0.,5.,0.2)   #values between 0 and 5 will be #generated with an interval of 0.2

plt.plot(x,x**2,'b--',label='power of 2')   #blue dashed lines plt.plot(x,x**3,'rs', label='power of 3')

#red squares formatting

plt.plot(x,x**4, 'g^', label='power of 4')

#green triangles formatting

plt.grid()

plt.legend()

#shows legends in the plot

plt.show()

Output

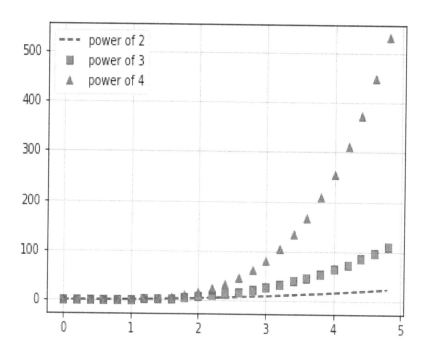

Example 12.5

Program

import matplotlib.pyplot as plt

x=[1,2,3,4]

y=[2,4,6,8]

plt.plot(x,y,linewidth=4.0)   #line width is specified as 4

plt.show()

Output

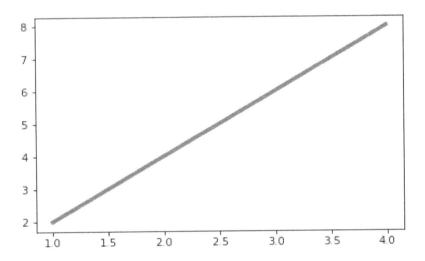

Example 12.6

Program

import matplotlib.pyplot as plt

```
x1=[1,2,3]

y1=[2,3,4]

x2=[1,2,3]

y2=[5,7,9]

lines=plt.plot(x1,y1,x2,y2)

 #the 2 plot lines are stored in lines list

plt.setp(lines[0],color='b', linewidth=4.0)

plt.setp(lines[1],color='g')
```

Output

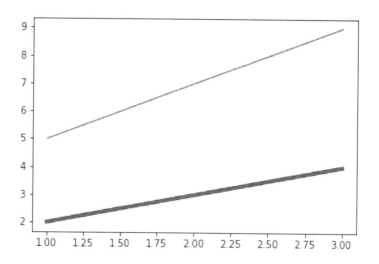

Example 12.7

Program

```
import matplotlib.pyplot as plt
```

```
plt.figure(1)                        # a figure is created
```

#divides the figure area into 2 rows and 1 column and #draws the first figure

```
plt.subplot(211)

plt.grid()

x1=[1,2,3]

y1=[2,4,6]

plt.plot(x1,y1,'b--')                #plots on the first figure
```

#divides the figure area into 2 rows, 1 column and draws #the second figure

```
plt.subplot(212)

plt.grid()

plt.plot([1,2,3],[5,10,15],'rs')  #plots on the second figure
```

Output

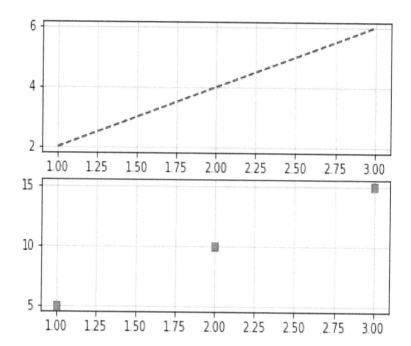

13.Numpy

- ➤ Numpy is the package for scientific computations.
- ➤ It is a general purpose array processing package.
- ➤ It has methods for working with arrays.
- ➤ Array class in Numpy is called as ndarray.
- ➤ Elements in Numpy arrays are indexed and can be accessed using square [] brackets.
- ➤ The number of dimensions of the array is called as rank of the array.
- ➤ Shape of the array denotes the size of the array in each dimension.
- ➤ Arrays can be initialised using lists.
- ➤ Numpy is memory and time efficient.
- ➤ 1D array is called vector, 2D array is called matrix and nD(3D,4D...nD) array is called Tensor.

13.1 ARRAY INITIALISATION AND INDEXING

For all the programs explained in this chapter, numpy has to be imported for successful execution.

Example 13.1

Program

```
import numpy as np

arr1=np.array([1,2,3])

print(arr1[2])          #prints the 3rd element in the array
```

Output

3

Example 13.2

Program

import numpy as np

array1=([1,2],[3,4])

print(array1[1][1])   #prints 2nd row, 2nd col element of
#the array

Output

4

Example 13.3

Program

import numpy as np

arr1=np.arange(6)   #initialises arr1 with values from 0 to 5

print(arr1)

Output

[0 1 2 3 4 5]

Example 13.4

Program

import numpy as np

arr1=np.ones(3)   #initialises array with shape 3 to 1

print(arr1)

Output

[1. 1. 1.]

Example 13.5

Program

```
import numpy as np

arr1=np.arange(0,50,5)   #initialises arr1 with values from
#0 to 49 in steps of 5

print(arr1)
```

Output

[0 5 10 15 20 25 30 35 40 45]

Example 13.6

Program

```
import numpy as np

arr1=np.linspace(0,1,5)

#start, end values and number of points

print(arr1)
```

Output

[0.   0.25 0.5 0.75 1.]

Example 13.7

Program

```
import numpy as np

arr1=np.arange(4*2*3).reshape(4,3,2)

#creating a 3D array

print(arr1)

print(arr1[3,2,1])
```

Output

```
[[[ 0  1]

  [ 2  3]

  [ 4  5]]

 [[ 6  7]

  [ 8  9]

  [10 11]]

 [[12 13]

  [14 15]

  [16 17]]


 [[18 19]

  [20 21]

  [22 23]]]

23          #output for arr1[3,2,1]
```

Example 13.8

Program

```
import numpy as np

arr1=np.array([[1,2,3],[3,4,5]])

print(arr1.ndim)        #prints the dimensions of the array
```

Output

```
2
```

Example 13.9

Program

```
import numpy as np

arr1=np.array([[1,2,3],[3,4,5]])

print(np.diag(arr1))

#extracts diagonal elements of matrix
```

Output

```
[1 4]
```

Example 13.10

Program

```
import numpy as np

arr1=np.array(["apple","mango","banana"])

 #string array
```

```
print(arr1[0])
```

Output

apple

We can create arrays for complex data types, float, boolean etc. also.

Example 13.11

Program

```
import numpy as np

arr1=np.arange(10)

#slicing the array (starting from 3rd  index) and values  will
#be made 5

arr1[3:]=5

print(arr1)
```

Output

[0 1 2 5 5 5 5 5 5 5]

Example 13.12

Program

```
import numpy as np

arr1=np.random.randint(0,10,15)

#creates an array with 15 values between 0 and 9

print(arr1)
```

Output

[7 7 2 8 9 1 7 3 1 4 0 5 1 2 8]

13.2 BASIC ARITHMETIC OPERATIONS

Example 13.13

Program

```
import numpy as np

array1=np.array([1,2,3])

print(array1+1)  #adds 1 to every element in the array
```

Output:

[2 3 4]

Example 13.14

Program

```
import numpy as np

arr1=np.array([10,20,30])

arr2=np.array([30,35,40])

print(arr1+arr2)   #adds 2 arrays elementwise
```

Output

[40 55 70]

Example 13.15

Program

```
import numpy as np

arr1=[10,20,30]

arr2=np.ones(3)   #initialises arr2 with shape 3 to 1

print(arr1+arr2)   #adds 2 arrays elementwise
```

Output

[11. 21. 31.]

Example 13.16

Program

```
import numpy as np

arr1=np.diag([2,4,6,8])

#creates a diagonal matrix with given diagonal elements

print(arr1*arr1)

#performs matrix multiplication of the diagonal matrices

print("\n")

print(arr1.dot(arr1))     #performs dot product
```

Output

[[4 0 0 0]

 [0 16 0 0]

 [0 0 36 0]

 [0 0 0 64]]

[[4 0 0 0]

 [0 16 0 0]

 [0 0 36 0]

 [0 0 0 64]]

13.3 BASIC COMPARISON OPERATIONS

Example 13.17

Program

```
import numpy as np

a=np.array([1,2,3])

b=np.array([2,3,4])

print(a==b)

#element wise comparison of two arrays

print(a<b)          #elementwise comparison

Output

[False False False]

[ True  True  True]
```

Example 13.18

Program

```
import numpy as np

a=np.array([1,2,3])
```

b=np.array([2,3,4])

c=np.array([2,3,4])

#compares 2 arrays and returns true if both are equal #element-wise

print(np.array_equal(a,b))

print(np.array_equal(b,c))

Output

False

True

13.4 LOGICAL OPERATIONS

Example 13.19

Program

import numpy as np

arr1=np.array([1,1,1,0],dtype=bool)

arr2=np.array([0,0,1,1],dtype=bool)

print(np.logical_or(arr1,arr2))

#logical OR operation element-wise

print(np.logical_and(arr1,arr2))

#logical AND operation element-wise

Output

[True True True True]

[False False True False]

Example 13.20

Program

import numpy as np

print(np.all([True, True, False]))

#returns True if all elements are True

print(np.all([True,True,True]))

Output

False

True

Example 13.21

Program

import numpy as np

print(np.any([True, True, False]))

#returns True if any one of the element is True

print(np.any([True,True,True]))

Output

True

True

Example 13.22

Program

```
import numpy as np

arr1=np.array([1,0,0])

print(np.any(arr1 != 0))

 #prints True if any of the element is not equal to 0

arr1=np.array([0,0,0])

print(np.any(arr1 != 0))
```

Output

True

False

Example 13.23

Program

```
import numpy as np

arr1=np.array([1,2,3])

#compares two array and returns True if both are equal
#element-wise

print(np.all(arr1 == arr1))
```

Output

True

13.5 COMBINING AND LOGICAL AND RELATIONAL OPERATORS

Example 13.24

Program

```
import numpy as np

arr1=np.array([1,2,3])

arr2=np.array([2,3,4])

arr3=np.array([3,4,5])

#performs element-wise comparison of arr1, arr2 and
#arr2, arr3  and performs logical AND.

# Then, returns True if all values in the list are True

print((((arr1<=arr2)&(arr2<=arr3)).all()))
```

Output

True

13.6 MATRIX TRANSPOSE

Example 13.25

Program

```
import numpy as np

arr1=np.array([[1,2,3],[4,5,6]])

arr1=arr1.T

print(arr1)
```

Output

[[1 4]

[2 5]

[3 6]]

13.7 FLATTENING AND RESHAPING

Flattening converts 2D array into 1D array.

Example 13.26

Program

```
arr1=np.array([[1,2,3],[4,5,6]])

print(arr1.ravel())
```

Output

[1 2 3 4 5 6]

Reshaping converts 1D array into 2D array.

Example 13.27

Program

```
arr1=np.array([[1,2,3],[4,5,6]])

print(arr1.ravel())          #converts 2D into 1D array

print(arr1.reshape(2,3))
```

#converts 1D to 2D(in this example 2 rows and 3 columns)
#array

Output

[1 2 3 4 5 6]

[[1 2 3]

 [4 5 6]]

13.8 TRANSCENDENTAL FUNCTIONS

Example13.28

Program

```
import numpy as np

arr1=np.array([0,1,2,3])

print(np.sin(arr1))

#calculates sin values for array elements
```

Output

[0.   0.84147098 0.90929743 0.14112001]

Example 13.29

Program

```
import numpy as np

arr1=np.array([0,1,2,3])

print(np.log(arr1))   #calculates log values
```

Output

[-inf 0.   0.69314718 1.09861229]

Example 13.30

Program

```
import numpy as np

arr1=np.array([0,1,2,3])

print(np.exp(arr1))

#calculates e^x for every element in array
```

Output

[1.   2.71828183 7.3890561 20.08553692]

13.9 REDUCTION OPERATIONS

Example 13.31

Program

```
import numpy as np

arr1=np.array([0,1,2,3])

print(arr1.sum())     #adds all elements in the array
```

Output

6

Example 13.32

Program

```
import numpy as np

array1=np.array([[1,2],[3,4]])
```

```
print(array1.sum(axis=0))
```

#prints sum of all elements column-wise in the array

```
print(array1.sum(axis=1))
```

#prints sum of all elements row-wise in the array

```
print(array1.min())
```

#prints minimum element in the array

```
print(array1.max())
```

#prints maximum element in the array

```
print(array1.argmax())
```

#prints the index value of maximum element in the array

```
print(array1.argmin())
```

#prints the index value of minimum element in the array

Output

[4 6]

[3 7]

1

4

3

0

13.10 | STATISTICAL OPERATIONS

Example 13.33

Program

```
import numpy as np

arr1=np.array([1,2,3])

print(arr1.mean())      #calculates mean
```

Output

```
2.0
```

Example 13.34

Program

```
import numpy as np

arr1=np.array([1,2,3,4,2])

print(np.median(arr1))    #calculates median

print(arr1.std())              #calculates standard deviation
```

Output

```
2.0

1.019803902718557
```

Example 13.35

Program

```
import numpy as np

arr1=np.array([[1,2,3],[3,4,5]])
```

print(np.median(arr1,axis=1))   #calculates row median

print(np.median(arr1,axis=0))   #calculates column median

Output

[2. 4.]

[2. 3. 4.]

13.11 BROADCASTING

➢ To perform arithmetic operations (addition, subtraction) on arrays that are of different sizes Broadcasting is used.
➢ Broadcasting describes how numpy treats arrays with different shapes during arithmetic operations.
➢ Subject to certain constraints, the smaller array is "broadcast" across the larger array so that they have compatible shapes and hence basic arithmetic operations(addition, subtraction) can be performed.

Example 13.36

Program

import numpy as np

arr1=np.array([1,2,3])

arr2=2

#the array elements will be broadcasted and arr2=[2,2,2]

print(arr1+arr2)

Output

[3 4 5]

Example 13.37

Program

import numpy as np

#arr1 will be tiled with 3 rows, values from 0 to 49 in steps #of 5

as it is (3,1) only row broadcasting occurs

arr1=np.tile(np.arange(0,50,5),(3,1))

print(arr1)

Output

[[0 5 10 15 20 25 30 35 40 45]

 [0 5 10 15 20 25 30 35 40 45]

 [0 5 10 15 20 25 30 35 40 45]]

Example 13.38

Program

import numpy as np

arr1=np.tile(np.arange(0,25,5),(3,2))

#row(thrice) and column(twice) broadcasting

print(arr1)

Output

[[0 5 10 15 20 0 5 10 15 20]

[0 5 10 15 20 0 5 10 15 20]

[0 5 10 15 20 0 5 10 15 20]]

Example 13.39

Program

import numpy as np

arr1=np.array([1,2,3])

print(arr1.shape)

arr1=arr1[:,np.newaxis]

#adds a new axis and so arr1 becomes 2D

print(arr1.shape)

Output

(3,)

(3, 1)→ 3 rows and 1 column

Example 13.40

The following program shows how broadcasting can help in performing addition of 2 matrices.

Program

import numpy as np

arr1=np.array([1,2,3])

arr1=arr1[:,np.newaxis]

arr2=np.array([3,4,5])

print(arr1+arr2)

Explanation for the program

In the above example, arr1 is converted to a 2D array using newaxis command. Hence, arr1 will be

[[1]

[2]

[3]]

Then, when it is added with arr2 which has [3,4,5] as elements, matrix addition will happen because of broadcasting. Column-wise broadcasting on arr1 and row-wise broadcasting of arr2 will result in

arr1=[[1 1 1]   arr2=[[3 4 5]

    [2 2 2]   [3 4 5]

    [3 3 3]]   [3 4 5]]

So the output would be

Output

[[4 5 6]

[5 6 7]

[6 7 8]]

13.12 SORTING

Example 13.41

Program

import numpy as np

arr1=np.array([[1,4,3],[9,7,8]])

arr2=np.sort(arr1,axis=1)   #row-wise sorting

print(arr2)

Output

[[1 3 4]

 [7 8 9]]

Example 13.42

Program

import numpy as np

arr1=np.array([1,4,3,2])

indices=np.argsort(arr1)

print(indices) #prints the indices of the sorted array

print(arr1[indices]) #prints the sorted array using indices

Output

[0 3 2 1]   #indices of 1,2, 3, 4 in arr1

[1 2 3 4]   #sorted array

14. Pandas

➢ Pandas, python module is widely used in machine learning projects.

➢ This library is extensively used in data analysis. Pandas facilitates easy analysis of data with lesser lines of code.

➢ Data frame is the main object (data structure) in Pandas. Data frame is used to represent data with rows and columns.

➢ This library can be installed using pip command.

In python3,

pip3 install pandas

command given in the command line installs pandas library.

Consider a csv (comma separated value) file being created for storing the stock details. Date, day high price, day low price are stored in the **share.csv** file. From this file a data frame data_fr is created as shown in the following example.

14.1 CREATION OF DATAFRAME

Example 14.1

Program

```
import pandas as pd

data_fr=pd.read_csv("share.csv")

print(data_fr)
```

Output

date high low

0 21-02-2019 152 148

1 22-02-2019 150 146

2 23-02-2019 150 147

3 24-02-2019 153 149

4 25-02-2019 165 156

5 26-02-2019 165 157

6 27-02-2019 162 156

7 28-02-2019 162 148

8 01-03-2019 157 152

9 02-03-2019 156 158

Similarly, data frame can be created from an excel file. xlrd module is to be installed for performing this operation. This can be done as follows.

pip3 install xlrd

Data frame can be created from excel file using the following command.

data_fr=pd.read_excel("share.xlsx")

If the data is to be stored in a csv file the following command is used.

data_fr.to_csv("share_copy.csv")

Data frame values will be stored in share_copy.csv file along with index values. To avoid this indexing, we can give the following command.

```
data_fr.to_csv("share_copy.csv",index=False)
```

Data frame values can be stored in excel file using the following command.

```
data_fr.to_excel("share_copy.xlsx",sheet_name="price")
```

Data frame can also be created using list of tuples. This is illustrated in the following example.

Example 14.2

Program

```
import pandas as pd

data_share=[('21-02-2019',152,148),('22-02-
2019',150,146),('23-02-2019',150,147),('24-02-2019',153,149)]
                    #list of tuples

data_fr=pd.DataFrame(data_share,columns=['date','high','
low'])

print(data_fr)
```

Output

```
    date  high  low

0  21-02-2019  152  148

1  22-02-2019  150  146

2  23-02-2019  150  147
```

3 24-02-2019   153 149

14.2 | BASIC OPERATIONS ON A DATAFRAME

Example 14.3 (shape)

Program

import pandas as pd

data_fr=pd.read_csv("share.csv")

print(data_fr.shape)

 #prints the number of rows and columns in the dataframe

Output

(10, 3)

Example 14.4 (head)

Program

import pandas as pd

data_fr=pd.read_csv("share.csv")

print(data_fr.head)

 #prints the top few rows in the dataframe

Output

<bound method NDFrame.head of   date high low

0 21-02-2019   152 148

1 22-02-2019   150 146

2 23-02-2019 150 147

3 24-02-2019 153 149

4 25-02-2019 165 156

5 26-02-2019 165 157

6 27-02-2019 162 156

7 28-02-2019 162 148

8 01-03-2019 157 152

9 02-03-2019 156 158>

data_fr.tail prints the bottom few rows in the dataframe.

14.3 ADVANCED OPERATIONS ON DATAFRAME

Example 14.5 (slice)

Program

import pandas as pd

data_fr=pd.read_csv("share.csv")

print(data_fr[2:5])   #slices the data starting from 2nd
#row till 4th row in the dataframe

Output

  date high low

2 23-02-2019 150 147

3 24-02-2019 153 149

4 25-02-2019 165 156

The dataframe created in Example 14.1 is used in the example programs (from 14.6 to 14.18). So, the code of these examples are to be appended with example 14.1 program code for successful execution.

Example 14.6

 Program

 print(data_fr.columns) #prints columns in the dataframe

 Output

Index(['date', 'high', 'low'], dtype='object')

Example 14.7

 Program

 print(data_fr.date)

 #return a dataframe with values in the column 'date'.

 # or

 print(data_fr['date'])

 #returns a dataframe with values in the column 'date'.

 Output

0 21-02-2019

1 22-02-2019

2   23-02-2019

3   24-02-2019

4   25-02-2019

5   26-02-2019

6   27-02-2019

7   28-02-2019

8   01-03-2019

9   02-03-2019

Example 14.8

Program

#returns dataframe with 'high' and 'low' column values

print(data_fr[['high','low']])

Output

   high low

0   152 148

1   150 146

2   150 147

3   153 149

4   165 156

5 165 157

6 162 156

7 162 148

8 157 152

9 156 158

Example 14.9

Program

print(data_fr['high'].max())

#highest value in the column 'high' is printed.

print(data_fr['high'].min())

#lowest value in the column 'high' is printed.

Output

165

150

Example 14.10

Program

#statistical parameters associated with 'high' column are #returned

print(data_fr['high'].describe())

Output

count   10.000000

mean   157.200000

std   5.940445

min   150.000000

25%   152.250000

50%   156.500000

75%   162.000000

max   165.000000

Name: high, dtype: float64

Example 14.11

Program

#prints the rows which have the maximum 'high' column value

print(data_fr[data_fr.high==data_fr.high.max()])

Output

date high low

4 25-02-2019 165 156

5 26-02-2019 165 157

Example 14.12

Program

#prints the dates which have the maximum 'high' column value

```
print(data_fr.date[data_fr.high==data_fr.high.max()])
```

Output

4   25-02-2019

5   26-02-2019

Name: date, dtype: object

Example 14.13

Program

```
print(data_fr.date[data_fr.high==152])
#returns the date on which 'high' is 152
```

Output

0   21-02-2019

Name: date, dtype: object

Example 14.14

Program

```
print(data_fr['high'].mean())
```

```
#mean value of the column 'high' is printed.
```

Output

157.2

14.4 GROUP-BY OPERATION

Example 14.15

Program

#groups the rows in dataframe (created from share.csv)
#based on 'high' column values.

high_val=data_fr.groupby('high')

#prints the 'high' column values and the dataframe
#corresponding to the 'high' column values

for high,high_df in high_val:

print(high)

print(high_df)

Output

150

date high low

1 2019-02-22 150 146

2 2019-02-23 150 147

152

date high low

0 2019-02-21 152 148

153

date high low

3 2019-02-24 153 149

156

```
    date  high  low
9 2019-03-02  156  158
157
```

```
    date  high  low
8 2019-03-01  157  152
162
```

```
    date  high  low
6 2019-02-27  162  156
7 2019-02-28  162  148
165
```

```
    date  high  low
4 2019-02-25  165  156
5 2019-02-26  165  157
```

Example 14.16

Program

```
#groups the dataframe based on column 'high'
high_val=data_fr.groupby('high')
# prints the dataframe for 'high' column value of 150
print(high_val.get_group(150))
```

Output

```
    date  high  low

1 2019-02-22  150  146

2 2019-02-23  150  147
```

Example 14.17

Program

#groups the dataframe based on column 'high' and

prints the row which has higher numerical values in columns(other than 'high')

in each group

high_val=data_fr.groupby('high')

print(high_val.max())

Output

```
high  date        low

150  2019-02-23  147

152  2019-02-21  148

153  2019-02-24  149

156  2019-03-02  158

157  2019-03-01  152

162  2019-02-28  156

165  2019-02-26  157
```

Example 14.18

Program

#groups the dataframe based on column 'high' and

#prints the mean value of the numerical values in

#columns(other than 'high') in each group

high_val=data_fr.groupby('high')

print(high_val.mean())

Output

high	low
150	146.5
152	148.0
153	149.0
156	158.0
157	152.0
162	152.0
165	156.5

14.5 CONCATENATE DATA FRAMES

The following example demonstrates the creation of 2 data frames using Dictionaries.

Example 14.19

Program

```
import pandas as pd

data_stud=pd.DataFrame({"name":["raj","ravi","anita"],"h
eight":[152,150,155],"weight":[75,62,55]})

print(data_stud)

data_stud1=pd.DataFrame({"name":["raghu","balu","jim"]
,"height":[182,160,175],"weight":[85,72,65]})

print(data_stud1)
```

Output

	name	height	weight
0	raj	152	75
1	ravi	150	62
2	anita	155	55

	name	height	weight
0	raghu	182	85
1	balu	160	72
2	jim	175	65

Now, these 2 dataframes can be concatenated as shown in the following example.

Example 14.20

Program

```
df=pd.concat([data_stud,data_stud1])

print(df)
```

Output

```
  name height weight

0  raj    152    75

1  ravi   150    62

2 anita   155    55

0 raghu   182    85

1 balu    160    72

2 jim     175    65
```

It is seen that when the 2 data frames are concatenated the indexing is not continuous and they donot reflect the row numbers. Following example illustrates the method to avoid this.

Example 14.21

Program

```
df=pd.concat([data_stud,data_stud1],ignore_index=True)

print(df)
```

Output

```
  name height weight

0  raj    152    75

1  ravi   150    62
```

2 anita   155   55

3 raghu   182   85

4 balu   160   72

5 jim   175   65

In the above example concatenation happens along the rows. In order to perform concatenation along the columns the following method is to be adopted.

Example 14.22

Program

df=pd.concat([data_stud,data_stud1],axis=1)

print(df)

Output

 name height weight name height weight

0 raj   152   75 raghu   182   85

1 ravi   150   62 balu   160   72

2 anita   155   55 jim   175   65

14.6 MERGING DATAFRAMES

2 dataframes can be merged using **merge** command. It is similar to **join** operation in databases. The first 2 examples illustrate the creation of 2 dataframes using dictionaries and the third example illustrates the merge operation.

Example 14.33

Program

import pandas as pd

data_stud=pd.DataFrame({"name":["raj","ravi","anita"],"h eight":[152,150,155]})

print(data_stud)

Output

```
  name  height

0  raj    152

1  ravi   150

2  anita  155
```

Example 14.34

Program

import pandas as pd

data_stud1=pd.DataFrame({"name":["raj","ravi"],"weight" :[85,72]})

print(data_stud1)

Output

```
  name  weight

0  raj    85

1  ravi   72
```

Merging of these 2 dataframes can be performed as shown in the following example.

Example 14.35

Program

```
df=pd.merge(data_stud,data_stud1,on="name")

print(df)
```

Output

```
name height  weight

0  raj    152     85

1  ravi   150     72
```

It is seen that the row with "name"="anita" is not included in the merge operation. This row will be included in the output by performing **outer join**. This is illustrated in the following example.

Example 14.36

Program

```
df=pd.merge(data_stud,data_stud1,on="name",how="out
er")

print(df)
```

Output

```
 name height  weight

0  raj    152   85.0

1  ravi   150   72.0
```

2 anita   155   NaN

14.7 NUMERICAL INDEXING IN DATAFRAMES

Normally, indices are generated for the dataframes automatically starting from value 0. Numerical indexing can be given by the user using **"index"** keyword while creating the dataframe. The creation of dataframes with numerical indices and accessing the frames using **loc, iloc** commands are explained using the following example.

Example 14.37

Program

```
import pandas as pd

#creating dataframe using user specified indices

df=pd.DataFrame([25,27,28,34],index=[12,13,14,0])

print("printing using loc ")

print(df.loc[14])

#returns the value present in the specified index position

print("printing using iloc")

print(df.iloc[2])

#returns the value present in the specified row
```

Output

```
printing using loc

0   28
```

Name: 14, dtype: int64

printing using iloc

0   28

Name: 14, dtype: int64

15.Summary

This book just scratched the surface of Python. Python has a massive support base thanks to the fact that it is open source and community developed. Millions of like-minded developers work with the language on a daily basis and continue to improve core functionality.

Python is used for backend Web Development, Data Analysis, Artificial Intelligence, and Scientific Computing. I hope that this book would have instilled your interest in Python programming. Keep updating your Python programming skills and all the best for your bright future.

ABOUT THE AUTHOR

V. Uma, is presently working as Assistant Professor in the Department of Computer Science, Pondicherry University. She received her M.Tech, and PhD degrees in Computer Science from Pondicherry University in 2007 and 2014 respectively. She was awarded the Pondicherry University gold medal for M.Tech. degree in Distributed Computing Systems. She has more than 12 years of teaching experience at Post Graduate level. Her research interest includes Machine Learning, Knowledge representation and reasoning (spatial and temporal knowledge) and Sentiment analysis. She has authored and co-authored more than 20 peer-reviewed journal papers. She has also authored 3 chapters in various books published by IGI Global. She has received the Best Paper Awards in International Conference on Digital Factory and International Conference on Smart Structures and Systems in the years 2008 and 2019 respectively.

www.ingramcontent.com/pod-product-compliance
Lightning Source LLC
Chambersburg PA
CBHW031241050326
40690CB00007B/899